OVERCOMING
DEPRESSION

BIBLE STUDY

HOPE FOR THE HEART BIBLE STUDIES

June Hunt

AspirePress

Hope For The Heart Bible Studies
Overcoming Depression Bible Study

© 2017 Hope For The Heart

Published by Aspire Press
an imprint of Hendrickson Publishing Group
Rose Publishing, LLC
P. O. Box 3473
Peabody, Massachusetts 01961-3473 USA
www.HendricksonPublishingGroup.com

ISBN 978-162862-390-1

The views and opinions expressed in this book are those of the author(s) and do not necessarily express the views of Rose Publishing, nor is this book intended to be a substitute for mental health treatment or professional counseling.

The information in this resource is intended as guidelines for healthy living. Please consult qualified medical, legal, pastoral, and psychological professionals regarding individual concerns.

For more information on Hope For The Heart, visit www.hopefortheheart.org or call 1-800-488-HOPE (4673).

Printed in the United States of America
May 2021, 4th printing

CONTENTS

About This Bible Study

THANK YOU. Sincerely. Thanks for taking the time and making the effort to invest in the study of God's Word with God's people. The apostle John wrote that he had "no greater joy than to hear that my children are walking in the truth" (3 John 4). At HOPE FOR THE HEART, our joy comes from seeing God use our materials to help His children walk in the truth.

OUR FOUNDATION

God's Word is our sure and steady anchor. We believe the Bible is *inspired* by God (He authored it through human writers), *inerrant* (completely true), *infallible* (totally trustworthy), and the *final authority* on all matters of life and faith. This study will give you *biblical* insight on the topic of depression.

WHAT TO EXPECT IN THIS BIBLE STUDY

The overall flow of this topical Bible study looks at depression from four angles: Definitions, Characteristics, Causes, and Biblical Steps to Solution.

- The DEFINITIONS section orients you to the topic by laying the foundation for a broad understanding of depression from a biblical and emotional standpoint. It answers the question: What does it mean?

- The CHARACTERISTICS section spotlights various aspects that are often associated with depression, giving a deeper understanding to the topic. It answers the question: What does it look like?

- The **CAUSES** section identifies the physical, emotional, and spiritual sources of depression. It answers the question: What causes it?

- The **BIBLICAL STEPS TO SOLUTION** sections provide action plans designed to help you—and help you help others—deal with depression from a scriptural point of view. It answers the question: What can you do about it?

The individual sessions contain narrative, biblical teaching, and discussion questions for group interaction and personal application. We sought to strike a balance between engaging content, biblical truth, and practical application.

GUIDELINES

Applying the following biblical principles will help you get the most out of this Bible-based study as you seek to live a life pleasing to the Lord.

- **PRAY** – "Unless the LORD builds the house, the builders labor in vain" (Psalm 127:1). Any progress in spiritual growth comes from the Lord's helping hand, so soak your study in prayer. We need to depend on God's wisdom to study, think, and apply His Word to our lives.

- **PREPARE** – Even ants prepare and gather food in the harvest (Proverbs 6:6–8). As with most activities in life, you will get out of it as much as you put into it. You will reap what you sow (Galatians 6:7). Realize, the more you prepare, the more fruit you produce.

- **PARTICIPATE** – Change takes place in the context of community. Come to each session ready to ask questions, engage with others, and seek God's help. And "do everything in love" (1 Corinthians 16:14).

- **PRACTICE** – James says, "Do not merely listen to the word, and so deceive yourselves. Do what it says" (James 1:22). Ultimately, this Bible study is designed to impact your life.

- **PASS IT ON!** – The Bible describes a spiritual leader who "set his heart to study the Law of the LORD, and to do it and to teach his statutes and rules" (Ezra 7:10 ESV). Notice the progression: *study . . . do . . . teach.* That progression is what we want for your journey. We pray that God will use the biblical truths contained in this material to change your life and then to help you help others! In this way, the Lord's work will lead to more and more changed lives.

OUR PRAYER

At HOPE FOR THE HEART, we pray that the biblical truths within these pages will give you the hope and help you need to handle the challenges in your life. And we pray that God will reveal Himself and His will to you through this study of Scripture to make you more like Jesus. Finally, we pray that God's Spirit will strengthen you, guide you, comfort you, and equip you to live a life that honors Jesus Christ.

A Note to Group Leaders

"Do your best to present yourself to God as one approved, a worker who does not need to be ashamed and who correctly handles the word of truth."

2 TIMOTHY 2:15

THANK YOU for leading this group. Your care and commitment to the members doesn't go unnoticed by God. Through this study, God will use you to do His work: to comfort, to encourage, to challenge, and even to bring people to saving faith in Christ. For your reference, we've included a gospel message on page 12 to assist you in bringing people to Christ. The following are some helpful tips for leading the sessions.

TIPS FOR LEADERS

- **PRAY** – Ask God to guide you, the members, and your time together as a group. Invite the group members to share prayer requests each week.

- **PREPARE** – Look over the sessions before you lead. Familiarize yourself with the content and find specific points of emphasis for your group.

- **CARE** – Show the members you are interested in their lives, their opinions, and their struggles. People will be more willing to share if you show them you care.

- **LISTEN** – Listen to the Lord's leading and the members' responses. Ask follow-up questions. A listening ear is often more meaningful than a good piece of advice.

- **GUIDE** – You don't have to "teach" the material. Your role is to *facilitate group discussion*: ask questions, clarify confusion, and engage the group members.

BEFORE THE FIRST MEETING

Schedule

- Determine the size of the group. Keep in mind that people tend to share more freely and develop genuine intimacy in smaller groups.

- Pick a time and place that works well for everyone.

- Decide how long each session will run. Sessions shouldn't take more than an hour or hour and a half.

- Gather the group members' contact information. Decide the best method of communicating (phone, text, email, etc.) with them outside of the group meeting.

Set Expectations

- **CONFIDENTIALITY** – Communicate that what is shared in the group needs to stay in the group.

- **RESPECTFULNESS** – Emphasize the importance of respecting each other's opinions, experiences, boundaries, and time.

- **PRAYER** – Decide how you want to handle prayer requests. If you take prayer requests during group time, factor in how much time that will take during the session. It may be more effective to gather requests on note cards during the sessions or have members email them during the week.

AT THE FIRST MEETING

Welcome

- Thank the members of your group for coming.

- Introduce yourself and allow others to introduce themselves.

- Explain the overall structure of study (Definitions, Characteristics, Causes, and Biblical Steps to Solution), including the discussion/application questions.

- Pray for God's wisdom and guidance as you begin this study.

LEADING EACH SESSION

Overview

- Summarize and answer any lingering questions from the previous session.

- Give a broad overview of what will be covered in each session.

How to Encourage Participation

- PRAY. Ask God to help the members share openly and honestly about their struggles. Some people may find it overwhelming to share openly with people they may not know very well. Pray for God's direction and that He would help build trust within the group.

- EXPRESS GRATITUDE AND APPRECIATION. Thank the members for coming and for their willingness to talk.

- **SPEAK FIRST.** The leader's willingness to share often sets the pace and depth of the group. Therefore, it is important that you, as the leader, begin the first few sessions by sharing from your own experience. This eases the pressure of the other members to be the first to talk. The group members will feel more comfortable sharing as the sessions progress. By the third or fourth session, you can ask others to share first.

- **ASK QUESTIONS.** Most of the questions in the study are open-ended. Avoid yes/no questions. Ask follow-up and clarifying questions so you can understand exactly what the members mean.

- **RESPECT TIME.** Be mindful of the clock and respectful of the members' time. Do your best to start and end on time.

- **RESPECT BOUNDARIES.** Some members share more easily than others. Don't force anyone to share who doesn't want to. Trust takes time to build.

Dealing with Difficulties

- You may not have an answer to every question or issue that arises. That's okay. Simply admit that you don't know and commit to finding an answer.

- Be assertive. Some people are more talkative than others, so it is important to limit the amount of time each person shares so everyone has a chance to speak. You can do this by saying something like: "I know this is a very important topic and I want to make sure everyone has a chance to speak, so I'm going to ask that everyone would please be brief when sharing." If someone tries to dominate the conversation, thank them for sharing, then invite others to speak. You can offer a non-condemning statement such as: "Good, thank you for sharing. Who else would like to share?" Or, "I'd like to make sure everyone has a chance to speak. Who would like to go next?"

- Sometimes people may not know how to answer a question or aren't ready to share their answer. Give the group time to think and process the material. Be okay with silence. Rephrasing the question can also be helpful.

- If someone misses a session, contact that person during the week. Let them know you noticed they weren't there and that you missed them.

WRAPPING UP

- Thank the group for their participation.

- Provide a brief summary of what the next session will cover.

- Encourage them to study the material for the next session during the week.

- Close in prayer. Thank God for the work He is doing in the group and in each person's life.

We are grateful to God for your commitment to lead this group. May God bless you as you guide His people toward the truth—truth that sets us free!

"If [your gift] is to lead,
do it diligently."

ROMANS 12:8

FOUR POINTS OF GOD'S PLAN

The gospel is central to all we do at Hope For The Heart. More than anything, we want you to know the saving love and grace of Jesus Christ. The following shows God's plan of salvation for you!

#1 GOD'S PURPOSE FOR YOU IS SALVATION.

God sent Jesus Christ to earth to express His love for you, save you, forgive your sins, empower you to have victory over sin, and to enable you to live a fulfilled life (John 3:16–17; 10:10).

#2 YOUR PROBLEM IS SIN.

Sin is living independently of God's standard—knowing what is right, but choosing what is wrong (James 4:17). The penalty of sin is spiritual death, eternal separation from God (Isaiah 59:2; Romans 6:23).

#3 GOD'S PROVISION FOR YOU IS THE SAVIOR.

Jesus died on the cross to personally pay the penalty for your sins (Romans 5:8).

#4 YOUR PART IS SURRENDER.

Place your faith in (rely on) Jesus Christ as your personal Lord and Savior and reject your "good works" as a means of earning God's approval (Ephesians 2:8–9). You can tell God that you want to surrender your life to Christ in a simple, heartfelt prayer like this: "God, I want a real relationship with You. Please forgive me for my sins. Jesus, thank You for dying on the cross to pay the penalty for my sins. Come into my life and be my Lord and Savior. In Your holy name I pray. Amen."

WHAT CAN YOU EXPECT NOW?

When you surrender your life to Christ, God empowers you to live a life pleasing to Him (2 Peter 1:3–4). Jesus assures those who believe with these words: "Very truly I tell you, whoever hears my word and believes him who sent me has eternal life and will not be judged but has crossed over from death to life" (John 5:24).

DEFINITIONS OF DEPRESSION

"Praise be to the Lord, to God our Savior,
who daily bears our burdens."

PSALM 68:19

Do you feel the weight of the world on your shoulders? Do you feel stuck in a painful situation, and you can't see the light at the end of the tunnel? Do you say to yourself, "I can't see anything that's good. I can't feel any happiness. I can't stop feeling so down." If so, like millions of people, you might be under the dark clouds of depression.

Depression doesn't discriminate. Men and women, young and old, rich and poor have struggled beneath the black clouds of depression. Can anything bring back the blue skies of contentment in the midst of depression?

King David of Israel discovered the answer to this question. He exchanged the darkness of despair for the light of God's hope.

> *"Why, my soul, are you downcast?*
> *Why so disturbed within me?*
> *Put your hope in God,*
> *for I will yet praise him,*
> *my Savior and my God."*
>
> Psalm 42:11

Write from the Heart

Read Psalm 42. How does David describe his depression and his relationship with God during his depression?

....

....

....

....

....

David found hope in bringing his difficult emotions to God. As a prayer to God, describe your experience (or that of a loved one) with depression. What was it like? What did you feel, think, and do during that time?

....

....

....

....

....

....

....

....

What Is Depression?

If you place a heavy iron on a heart-shaped pillow, the buoyant pillow becomes pressed down—"depressed." But if you remove the iron the next day, the pillow pops right back to its original form. However, if you wait to remove the iron for months, the pillow will not spring back to its original shape. Instead, it will be flat and stay depressed. A pillow, which can sustain temporary pressure, is not designed to hold its shape for long under heavy pressure.

The same is true for the human heart. When it is "pressed down" due to normal pressure from normal situations (situational depression), your heart is able to rebound after the pressure is removed. However, you were not designed to live under the weight of heavy pressure for long periods of time. During those painful times when hope seems elusive, your emotions feel flat and your heart feels sick.

The Bible explains . . .

"Hope deferred makes
the heart sick."
Proverbs 13:12

DEFINITIONS OF DEPRESSION

- Depression is a condition of being literally "pressed down" to a lower position (as in a footprint).[1]

- Depression can refer to a state of decline and reduced activity (as in an economic depression).[2]

The apostle Paul used the Greek word *bareo*, which means "pressed or weighed down," to describe the immense emotional pressure and severe hardships that he and Timothy suffered at the hands of those who opposed Christ.[3]

"We do not want you to be uninformed, brothers and sisters, about the troubles we experienced in the province of Asia.

We were under great pressure, far beyond our ability to endure, so that we despaired of life itself.

Indeed, we felt we had received the sentence of death."

2 CORINTHIANS 1:8–9

What Is Psychological Depression?

In ancient writings, the earliest reference for our word *depression* was the word *melancholia* (literally "black bile"). The assumption was that the melancholy person had an excess of black bile, which resulted in depression.

In the second century AD, a physician named Aretaeus referred to his melancholy patients as "sad, dismayed, sleepless. They become thin by their agitation and loss of refreshing sleep. At a more advanced state, they complain of a thousand futilities and desire death."[4]

Today, melancholia is defined as "a mental condition characterized by extreme depression, bodily complaints, and often hallucinations and delusions."[5]

Psychology is the science or study of the mind as it relates to thoughts, feelings, and behaviors, focusing on why people think, feel, and act as they do.[6] Thus, the term *psychological depression* pertains to the mental, emotional, and behavioral characteristics of a depressed person. Psychological depression is a state in which the heart is pressed down and unable to experience joy. It is an umbrella term that covers feelings from mild discouragement to intense despair.[7] Those suffering with depression can feel trapped underneath a pervasive canopy of sadness, grief, guilt, and hopelessness.

But even though those suffering may *feel* hopeless, there is hope. God is the "God of hope" (Romans 15:13). The Bible says Jesus Christ is "our hope" (1 Timothy 1:1).

You can be confident that . . .

> *"There is surely a future hope for you,*
> *and your hope will not be cut off."*
> PROVERBS 23:18

God is the "God of hope."

Romans 15:13

Write from the Heart

What promises in God's Word give you hope in seemingly hopeless situations? Pick one or two and commit them to memory. Consider: Psalm 40:1–4; Isaiah 41:10; Jeremiah 29:11; Lamentations 3:21–24; Romans 8:18, 37–39; 2 Corinthians 4:16–18.

Four Classic Types of Psychological Depression

1. NORMAL DEPRESSION:
Situational or Reactive Depression

- An involuntary reaction to painful pressure.

- The normal problems of life press down the heart for a short period of time (rejection, failure, illness).

- The transitional stages of life often press the heart down (adolescence, empty nest, grief over losing a loved one, midlife crises, major moves, menopause, retirement).

- Some common signs of normal depression include:
  - Self-doubt
  - Worry
  - Fear
  - Forgetfulness
  - Anger
  - Sadness
  - Diminished joy
  - Irritability
  - Activity pattern upset
  - Loss of appetite
  - Sleep difficulty
  - No thoughts of suicide

2. MASKED DEPRESSION:
Hidden Depression

- A state of buried unresolved conflict.

- True painful feelings are denied or covered up.

- Relief from pain is unconsciously found in self-effort or excessive activity.

- Some common signs of masked depression include:
  - Self-inflation
  - Appearance of invincibility
  - Disorganized thoughts
  - Suppressed anger
  - Distraction
  - Self-sacrifice
  - Judgmentalism
  - Increased activity
  - Weight gain
  - Less need for sleep
  - Unspoken thoughts of suicide

3. NEUROTIC DEPRESSION:
A Minor Depressive Disorder[8]

- A prolonged state of depression (longer than the normal time frame needed for emotional recovery).

- The symptoms interfere with normal biological and social activities.

- The cause can usually be traced to a precipitating event.

- Some common signs of neurotic depression include:
  - Self-criticism
  - Hypochondria
  - Inability to make decisions
  - Anger
  - Hopelessness
  - No pleasure
  - Apathy
  - Diminished activity
  - Weight loss
  - Escape by sleeping
  - Manipulation by threatening suicide

4. PSYCHOTIC DEPRESSION: A Major Depressive Disorder[9]

- A severe state of depression.

- A psychosis involves dissociation or a loss of contact with reality.

- The psychotic person can experience hallucinations, delusions, and/or schizophrenia.

- Some common signs of psychotic depression include:
  - Self-rejection
  - Hallucinations
  - Lack of judgment or reasoning
  - Acute anger
  - Schizophrenia
  - No pleasure
  - Unresponsiveness
  - Catatonia
  - Weight loss
  - Severe insomnia
  - Severe threat of suicide

Depression and Sin

How are depression and sin related? Is depression a sin? This is an often-asked question. No, depression is not always related to sin. As you will discover in this study, there are a variety of reasons why a person may experience depression. Yet, depression can be the byproduct of sin in the following circumstances.[10]

- Depression becomes sin when you are depressed over the consequences of your sin and make no attempt to change. (See 2 Corinthians 7:10.)

- Depression becomes sin when you use it to manipulate others.

- Depression becomes sin when you hold on to self-pity and anger.

- Depression becomes sin when you continually blame God and others for your unhappiness.

How you respond to your hurts and losses in life is important. Jesus cares about your heart and knows you are especially vulnerable to depression when you are heavyhearted. The Lord encourages you in His Word to cast your burdens and anxieties on Him.

"Cast all your anxiety on him because He cares for you."

1 PETER 5:7

BIBLICAL EXAMPLE
The Book of Jonah

The Old Testament prophet Jonah is an example of reactive depression as a result of sin. God calls Jonah to preach, but he disobeys God and ends up angry and depressed. (Read about Jonah's descent into depression in the book of Jonah, chapters 1–4.)

- *Chapter 1: Disobedience*

  The Lord appoints Jonah to preach repentance to the godless people of Nineveh. But Jonah rebels and boards a ship going in a different direction. When Jonah's disobedience brings repercussions on the ship's crew, he is rejected and literally thrown overboard.

- *Chapter 2: Dread*

  Recognizing that he is about to lose his life inside the belly of a great fish, Jonah cries out for mercy. The Lord extends mercy and spares his life.

- *Chapter 3: Declaration*

  Jonah resigns himself to obey God's call. He declares God's truth, and all of Nineveh repents.

- *Chapter 4: Depression*

  Jonah becomes angry with God for extending mercy to those whom he doesn't deem worthy of mercy. Ultimately, Jonah becomes consumed with anger, bitterness, self-pity, and despair to the extent of wanting to die. He even states, "I'm so angry I wish I were dead" (Jonah 4:9).

Write from the Heart

What does the story of Jonah teach you about the relationship between sin and depression? What did Jonah desire more than doing God's will? In what ways do you relate to Jonah?

Discussion/Application Questions

1. What are common misconceptions about depression? What makes this topic difficult to discuss?

2. Sometimes Christians feel *guilt* when they're depressed, and often that guilt is fueled by other Christians who consider depression a sin. How would you respond to someone who says depression is a sin?

3. Read Psalm 55:22; Matthew 11:28–29; 1 Peter 5:7. What does the Lord want you to do with your burdens? What does He promise He will do?

4. Is there anyone in your life who is currently struggling with depression or heavy burdens? Write down the names of those you can pray for and encourage this week. What are some practical things you can do for them or Scriptures you can share with them?

5. Psalm 68:19 says, "Praise be to the Lord, to God our Savior, who daily bears our burdens." The psalmist praises God for bearing his burdens—*daily*. Take time right now to praise God and express your gratitude to Him. Write down the reasons for which you can praise and thank God.

Notes

"Now may the Lord of peace himself give you
peace at all times and in every way."
2 Thessalonians 3:16

SESSION 2

CHARACTERISTICS OF DEPRESSION

"For we do not have a high priest who is unable to empathize with our weaknesses, but we have one who has been tempted in every way, just as we are—yet he did not sin. Let us then approach God's throne of grace with confidence, so that we may receive mercy and find grace to help us in our time of need."

HEBREWS 4:15–16

The Common Thread in Depression

On June 20, 2001, the nation struggled to comprehend the shocking news: Andrea Yates of Houston, Texas, had systematically drowned her children in the bathtub—all five of them, ranging in age from six months to seven years.[11]

The question on everyone's mind was repeated: *How could a mother do the unthinkable—kill her own children? What could drive a mother to commit such a heinous crime?*

Depression. Yet in Andrea's case, it was not "normal depression," but was rather a psychotic depression that caused her to break with reality.[12]

The media quickly learned that this rigidly religious family had been dealing with Andrea's severe depression for several years. The newspapers reported that in 1999 she had attempted suicide twice. And because of her severe postpartum depression following the birth of their fourth son, the couple was also advised to have no more children—yet a fifth child was born.

The Yates' situation is certainly not the norm. The majority of those who experience common depression will never experience the type of depression that led to such devastation. Yet the common thread in all types of depression is a sense of hopelessness.

Write from the Heart

Hopelessness fuels depression. List some common experiences that can cause people to feel hopeless and depressed. What causes you to feel this way?

....

....

....

....

....

....

Read Lamentations 3:19–26. What was the writer feeling when he wrote this (vv. 19–20), and what gave him hope (vv. 21–26)?

....

....

....

....

....

....

Navigating the Negatives

At one time or another everyone experiences normal depression. You sometimes get "the blues" when life doesn't go as planned or when physical exhaustion leaves you drained of your natural ability to rebound from disappointments. Physical problems may be getting you down. Losses and hurts may be stealing your joy. During these times, it is common for people to mask their real feelings, closing off authentic intimacy with others and even with the Lord. However, failure to confront your feelings with honesty can lead to symptoms associated with depressive disorders.

You can work through your painful and difficult feelings by spending time with the Lord and by becoming involved in a biblical community—in a church, in a small group, and through the study of His Word. This may take weeks and months, but if you heed the danger signs and work through your painful feelings, you can avoid needless and excessive suffering.

> "The righteous cry out, and the LORD
> hears them; he delivers them
> from all their troubles."
>
> PSALM 34:17

Those who struggle in the darkness of depression have difficulty seeing the good in their circumstances and in themselves. They look at life through a "day for night" filter. The photographer who uses a day for night filter can take a picture during the daytime, but the final photograph will appear to be a night scene. Those who battle depression often see life through a filter of darkness, feeling hatred toward themselves, feeling helpless about their situation, and feeling hopeless about their future.

If you are walking in the darkness of depression and it seems that no one cares, be assured—God cares.

"The LORD is gracious and compassionate, slow to anger and rich in love. The LORD is good to all; he has compassion on all he has made."

PSALM 145:8–9

Write from the Heart

Those who battle depression often see life through a filter of darkness. Describe what that means to you.

. . . .

. . . .

. . . .

. . . .

. . . .

. . . .

Spending time in the Bible often removes the filter and allows the light of God's truth to shine through. Write out a passage of Scripture that encourages you each time you read it. Challenge yourself to commit it to memory. Consider: Psalm 23:1–4; 119:50, Isaiah 40:31, John 14:27.

. . . .

. . . .

. . . .

. . . .

. . . .

. . . .

The Dialogue of the Depressed

It's very likely that you're familiar with the dialogue of the depressed. You may hear it in a child or in your spouse. The dialogue may repeat in your mind. People tend to speak what they feel. Jesus said, "for the mouth speaks what the heart is full of" (Luke 6:45).

It's a challenge to rise above condemning and critical thoughts when you are feeling blue. Yet for every negative thought you may have, God's Word counters with His loving reminders.

"One thing God has spoken,
two things I have heard:
'Power belongs to you, God,
and with you, lord,
is unfailing love.'"

PSALM 62:11–12

What you say about yourself:

- "I can't do anything right."

- "Why try?"

- "I'm no longer useful."

- "I hate myself."

- "Look at so-and-so (by comparison)."

- "I must have done something wrong."

- "Nobody loves me."

What is the light of truth?

> The Lord says, "I have loved you with an everlasting love; I have drawn you with unfailing kindness" (Jeremiah 31:3).

What you say about your situation:

- "I don't see any way out."

- "It doesn't matter anyway."

- "I can't do anything about it."

- "I can't bear it; it's intolerable."

- "It's not fair."

- "I'm helpless to change it."

What is the light of truth?

> I can say with Paul, "I can do all things through Christ who strengthens me" (Philippians 4:13 NKJV).

What you say about your future:

- "Who cares?"

- "Nothing will change."

- "It's hopeless."

- "No one will ever love me."

- "I'll be too old."

- "That was my last chance for happiness."

- "I have nothing to live for."

What is the light of truth?

The psalmist prays, "Send me your light and your faithful care, let them lead me" (Psalm 43:3).

You're Not the Only One

Sometimes depression can make you *feel* like everyone's life is going along smoothly—everyone's except yours. Some who experience bouts of depression surmise that it's because they just aren't good enough Christians. Does that sound like you?

The classic biblical example of depression is David. His depression can be found in the Bible's longest book, Psalms. (See chapters 6, 13, 18, 23, 25, 27, 31–32, 34, 37–40, 42–43, 46, 51, 55, 62–63, 69, 71, 73, 77, 84, 86, 90–91, 94–95, 103–104, 107, 110, 116, 118, 121, 123–124, 130, 138–139, 141–143, 146–147.)

Within the pages of Scripture, you will find others who battled depression:

- Abraham (see Genesis chapter 15)

- Job (see the book of Job)

- Elijah (see 1 Kings chapter 19)

- Jeremiah (see the book of Jeremiah)

- Jonah (see Jonah chapter 4)

- King Saul (see 1 Samuel 16:14–23)

Discussion/Application Questions

1. Think of a character or two in the Bible who struggled with depression. In what ways can you relate to them?

....

....

....

....

....

....

....

2. How easily can you recognize patterns of depression in others? In your child? In a friend? In your spouse? What can you *do* or *say* to help prevent or alleviate their downward spiral of depression?

....

....

....

....

....

....

3. Have you put yourself on your own prayer list? Do you remember to pray for everyone else, but seem to forget to pray for yourself? God's ear is always open. If you could request one thing for yourself from God right now, what would that be?

Have you put yourself on your own prayer list?

Notes

Notes

"Now may the Lord of peace himself give you peace at all times and in every way."
2 Thessalonians 3:16

SESSION 3

CAUSES OF
DEPRESSION

*"He [God] has rescued us from the dominion of
darkness and brought us into the kingdom
of the Son he loves, in whom we have
redemption, the forgiveness of sins."*

COLOSSIANS 1:13–14

A Unique Situation, A Common Enemy

Andrea Yates suffered from postpartum depression long before her fifth child. About 60–70 percent of birth mothers experience a mild depression called the "baby blues" (unexplained crying, mood swings, and irritability). These symptoms usually subside after a few weeks. However, 5–20 percent experience postpartum depression, which is distinguished from the "baby blues" both by its long duration and the debilitating indifference of the mother toward herself and her children.[13]

But Andrea's condition was worse than most. She was struggling with *postpartum psychosis* (a break with reality). This psychotic disorder affects one or two out of every 1,000 birth mothers.[14] Many of these mothers with postpartum psychosis are consumed with thoughts of harming their babies and themselves. Andrea became suicidal and was hospitalized.

Andrea was also spiritually unbalanced. She had a greater focus on Satan and sin than on God and grace. She spoke of seeing visions and hearing voices. She claimed that she was evil. She spoke about Satan influencing her. She thought the only way to stop his influence was for her to die . . . and do something deserving of the death penalty.[15]

Andrea's situation was unique, but Scripture is clear: The enemy of God, the devil, seeks to harm people. This is why it is important to stand firm in the faith.

Write from the Heart

Read 1 Peter 5:8–9. What does it mean to "stand firm in the faith"? What helps you do that? Describe the difference regular Bible reading, prayer, and church fellowship makes (or can make) in your life.

Physical Contributors

Changes in the body can lead to depression. These include thyroid deficiency or hormonal changes during puberty, postpartum (after childbirth), and perimenopause (around menopause).

Genetics can also play a role. People who have had depressed, close family members are two times more vulnerable to depression.[16] Half of those with bipolar disorder have at least one parent with the disorder.[17]

Gender is also a factor. More women suffer from depression than men. Women produce half the amount of serotonin men do; however, estrogen in women multiplies the amount of serotonin to equal the level in men. Prior to a woman's menstrual cycle, after childbirth, and around menopause, estrogen levels drop, sometimes severely. When a woman's estrogen level is not sufficient to multiply serotonin, she experiences a depletion of serotonin, which can cause depression. This is one reason many women receive Estrogen Replacement Therapy (ERT).[18]

Six Physical Contributors to Depression

1. Hormonal imbalance
2. Medications and drugs
3. Chronic illnesses
4. Melancholy temperament
5. Improper food, rest, exercise
6. Genetic vulnerability

Depression also affects the brain.[19] Medical research verifies that some people have a condition in the brain called hippocampal atrophy, which results from a chemical imbalance (for example, too much or too little adrenal cortisol) in the hippocampus region of the brain. During these states of depression the hippocampus physically shrinks.

Emotional Causes

Emotions can play a factor in depression, especially when not handled properly. When you neglect or repress your difficult emotions, you can harm yourself and your relationships. Anger, for example, is a normal emotion of irritation or agitation, occurring when a need or expectation is not met.[20] Everyone experiences anger, but repressed anger is anger that has been hidden or held on to for a long time. It often involves bitterness, resentment, or fear.[21] Failure to adequately express your emotions can contribute to depression. And in today's broken world, numerous things can lead people to become angry, fearful, or stressed.

Repressed anger over:

- Loss of a loved one
- Loss of control
- Loss of expectations
- Loss of health or abilities
- Loss of self-esteem
- Loss of possessions
- Loss of respect for others
- Loss of personal goals

Suppressed fear of:

- Losing a job
- Empty nest
- Abandonment
- Being alone

- Dying
- Failure
- Growing old
- Rejection

Internalized stress over:

- New job
- Marital problems
- Financial obligations
- Troubled child
- Relocation
- Workload
- Family responsibilities
- Alcoholic spouse

So what do you do with these stresses and emotions? God repeatedly commands us to get rid of emotions like anger and bitterness: "Get rid of all bitterness, rage and anger . . . " (Ephesians 4:31).

But how do you "get rid" of these emotions? It does not mean that you neglect your emotions; it means that you express them appropriately. This is a process that takes time and is accomplished with the Lord's help. He is willing to help and hear you when you come to Him. God wants you to come to Him with whatever you are feeling. In fact, the psalms repeatedly show how people bring their difficult emotions to the Lord . . .

*"I cry aloud to the L*ORD*; I lift up my voice to the L*ORD *for mercy. I pour out before him my complaint; before him I tell my trouble."*

PSALM 142:1–2

Spiritual Sources

Just as there are physical and emotional reasons for depression, there are also spiritual reasons for a despairing heart.

Sin

King David felt physically and emotionally weak when he kept silent about his sin (Psalm 32:3–4). After confessing his guilt, God forgave him and he was moved to *rejoice* in the Lord (Psalm 32:5, 11).

"Then I acknowledged my sin to you and did not cover up my iniquity. I said, 'I will confess my transgressions to the LORD.' And you forgave the guilt of my sin" (Psalm 32:5).

Longing for God

Sometimes sin and disobedience are not the issue. Sometimes God's people show signs of depression because they intensely long for God's presence.

In Psalm 42, David writes about his downcast soul due to his deep desire for God. He pants and thirsts for God (vv. 1–2). He writes that his "tears have been my food day and night" (v. 3). He repeatedly asks himself why he is so downcast (vv. 5, 11). He mourns (v. 9), and even his bones are in agony (v.10). His experience is not a result of sin or disobedience but actually due to his longing for God (vv. 1–2).

"As the deer pants for streams of water, so my soul pants for you, my God. My soul thirsts for God, for the living God" (Psalm 42:1–2).

The Devil

Lastly, the influence of the devil and dark spiritual forces can be a source of depression. Jesus called Satan a murderer and a liar (John 8:44). He is elsewhere called "the accuser" (Revelation 12:10). He is compared to a lion seeking to devour people (1 Peter 5:8). As the enemy of God, he does not want people to delight in God (Psalm 37:4) or experience the full joy of their salvation (Psalm 51:12). His attacks and accusations must be fought with the Word of God.

"Finally, be strong in the Lord and in his mighty power. Put on the full armor of God, so that you can take your stand against the devil's schemes. For our struggle is not against flesh and blood, but against the rulers, against the authorities, against the powers of this dark world and against the spiritual forces of evil in the heavenly realms. Therefore put on the full armor of God, so that when the day of evil comes, you may be able to stand your ground, and after you have done everything, to stand. Stand firm then, with the belt of truth buckled around your waist, with the breastplate of righteousness in place, and with your feet fitted with the readiness that comes from the gospel of peace. In addition to all this, take up the shield of faith, with which you can extinguish all the flaming arrows of the evil one. Take the helmet of salvation and the sword of the Spirit, which is the word of God. And pray in the Spirit on all occasions with all kinds of prayers and requests. With this in mind, be alert and always keep on praying for all the Lord's people." —EPHESIANS 6:10–18

Write from the Heart

Of the physical, emotional, and spiritual contributors to depression listed in this section, which ones have you experienced? What experiences or emotions have you "stuffed down" or neglected, hoping they would go away on their own? What was the result of doing that?

Who can you talk to when you are dealing with difficult emotions? List the names of any trusted family members, friends, pastors, or counselors. Do you need to reach out to one of them for something you are currently dealing with?

What to Say to Yourself When You Are Stuck in Situational Depression

Wrong Belief	Right Belief
"The failures, losses, and disappointments in my life have robbed me of all joy. There's no hope for my future, and there's nothing I can do about it."	"I admit I am depressed over the circumstances in my life. But in Christ, I have hope. I will choose to renew my mind with God's Word and do whatever I need to do in order to experience the future He planned for me."

"For everything that was written in the past was written to teach us, so that through the endurance taught in the Scriptures and the encouragement they provide we might have hope."

Romans 15:4

Discussion/Application Questions

1. The things we expose ourselves to can affect our mood. In what ways do books, TV shows, movies, video games, Internet, and social media impact people's mood? Describe the benefits and dangers of these types of media.

2. The Lord wants you to love Him with all your mind. (Read Matthew 22:37.) Look again at the wrong belief/right belief box in this session. What reoccurring *wrong beliefs* do you struggle with? What *right beliefs* from God's Word can you replace them with?

....

....

....

....

....

....

3. God desires that you honor Him with your body (1 Corinthians 6:20). What physical changes can you make that would lead to a better sense of well-being and health? What habits need to start, stop, or change?

....

....

....

....

....

....

....

....

....

....

....

....

....

....

4. The Lord commands us to "bear one another's burdens" (Galatians 6:2). Think about those in your life who are burdened or even depressed. How can you best love them this week? (Simply listening to their struggles or being a calming presence can make a big difference.)

....

....

....

....

....

....

....

Notes

"Now may the Lord of peace himself give you
peace at all times and in every way."
2 Thessalonians 3:16

SESSION 4

BIBLICAL STEPS TO SOLUTION
PART 1

"Call on me in the day of trouble; I will deliver you, and you will honor me."

PSALM 50:15

Grace When You Need It Most

Were the family and friends of Andrea Yates aware of the seriousness of her depression?[22]

Many people wondered if Andrea's husband, Rusty, did enough to ensure his wife's safety and the safety of their children. Answers to these questions became apparent in the court trial. Rusty admitted Andrea to institutions for her severe depression several times. She was released twice.[23] He made an appeal to her last doctor, stating that Andrea needed the medication prescribed in the past, which seemed to work. His appeal was denied because of the adverse side effects of the medication.[24]

Rusty eventually developed and initiated a schedule to ensure Andrea had help. Rusty left for work every morning at 9:00. His mother came to the house every morning at 10:00 to help Andrea with the children. Andrea would be alone with the children for *only one hour* each day. But during that *one hour* on June 20, 2001, Andrea carried out each drowning.

If only. How many times have you had that thought? *If only* you could turn back the hands of time. Surely, Andrea's family was left to wonder what could have been done to move her from the darkness of despair to the light of hope. When your questions are overwhelming, you can approach God with confidence and expect His mercy and grace when you need it most.

Write from the Heart

Read Psalm 10:1; 13:1; 42:9. What did the psalmist ask God in these verses? What do you think the writer was feeling when he wrote these questions?

....

....

....

....

....

....

....

Now read Psalm 3:4; 50:15. The psalms are filled with questions directed at God and answers from Him. What burning questions do you have for God? What answers does His Word provide for your questions?

....

....

....

....

....

Dealing with Depression: Body, Soul, and Spirit

Depression affects the whole person:

- Body

- Soul (mind, will, emotions)

- Spirit

It's important to recognize the subtle ways depression slips in almost without notice, leaving its calling card of gloom. In this session, you will discover how you can you protect yourself against this damaging invasion.

GROOM THE BODY

- Schedule a thorough medical checkup. Tell your doctor if you've felt depressed.

- Ask your doctor to evaluate all the medications you take to see if any might be contributing to your depression.

- Develop regular sleeping habits. Sleep enables the brain to produce serotonin, which alleviates depression. Avoid becoming overly-fatigued.

- Maintain a regular schedule of activity and exercise at least four days a week. A brisk 20-minute walk releases endorphins, a natural mood elevator.

- Eat balanced, nutritious meals regularly.

- Take time each day for a stress-relieving activity such as walking, praying, listening to music, or journaling.

Write from the Heart

When you're feeling down, what do you do to feel better? What activities help you relieve the "blues"?

What is . . .
Seasonal Affective Disorder (SAD)?

Seasonal Affective Disorder (SAD) is a form of depression associated with deprivation of sunlight.[25] SAD typically begins in the fall season with shorter days and less sunlight, and subsides in the spring, as the days get longer. Symptoms include excessive sleep, lethargy, overeating, and depression. If you think you might have SAD, check with your healthcare professional about a diagnosis and treatment options.

GUARD THE SOUL

It takes time. When you've lost a significant relationship, whether by rejection, divorce, or death, it's quite normal for your heart to become weighted down. With the passage of time, the weight of depression usually eases, but it takes time—sometimes months or even years. But if your heart continues to maintain its heaviness, you may be in a state of depression.

Since the entire soul (mind, will, and emotions) is affected by depression, recovery involves taking steps to treat all three areas of the soul. Each part that has been touched by depression needs to be reached with healing.

1. The Mind

2. The Will

3. The Emotions

1. The Mind

Research shows that a person's thoughts literally change the chemistry of the brain. As you fill your mind with God's Word, you will become filled with His perspective and promises. Romans 12:2 says that you are, "transformed by the renewing of your mind."

But what does this really mean? How can you *renew* your mind?

- Write several Scriptures on index cards and read them several times a day. For example, you could start with Psalm 18:28; 23:1–3; Romans 8:1, 37–39; Ephesians 2:8–10.

- Make a list (My Thanksgiving List) of seven good things in your life, and spend time every day thanking God for those things. During the next week, add seven more things to your list that you are thankful for and thank God for those. Keep adding to the list each week.

Searching God's Word can help you discover God's purpose for allowing the painful losses in your life. You may not understand them fully, and that's okay. Always remember, God has a purpose in all things—even in the storms in your life.

> *"Be joyful in hope, patient in affliction,*
> *faithful in prayer."*
>
> Romans 12:12

Write from the Heart

To get started on your Thanksgiving List, write down seven things for which you are grateful.

(1) ....

....

(2) ....

....

(3) ....

....

(4) ....

....

(5) ....

....

(6) ....

....

(7) ....

....

2. The Will

Do you ever *want* to do something but that's as far as you get? Do you sometimes experience paralysis of the will? People with prolonged depression sometimes feel this way. Life comes with unavoidable challenges, but God's presence and God's Word can help guide us to make the right choices and avoid needless discouragement.

> *"Yet I am always with you; you hold me by my right hand. You guide me with your counsel, and afterward you will take me into glory."*
>
> PSALM 73:23–24

Choose to rely on Him for the power to accomplish your goals. Sometimes the smallest changes can be the most helpful in freeing the paralysis of your will. Try these suggestions:

- Keep your living environment bright, cheerful, and uncluttered.

- Watch less television. Listen to uplifting and inspirational music.

- Set small, attainable goals every day. Take a daily walk, for instance.

- Write thank-you and encouragement notes to others.

- Look for ways to help someone each day.

> *"Do not let your hearts be troubled. You believe in God; believe also in me."*
>
> JOHN 14:1

Write from the Heart

What are some things you can change in your environment that
would make your living or work space more cheerful?

What are some small, achievable goals you can set that would add joy
to your daily life?

3. The Emotions

Often, people who are depressed have difficulty expressing their feelings in a healthy way. A common cause of depression is buried feelings due to loss or past hurts. The result is like poison to your emotions. That's why it's vital to face your feelings. Bring your heartache and hurts, your anxiety and anger, your fear and frustration to Jesus and receive His comfort. He alone understands the depth of your pain.

The Bible assures us . . .

> *"The Lord is a refuge for the oppressed,*
> *a stronghold in times of trouble."*
>
> Psalm 9:9

What is . . .
Anniversary Depression?

Anniversary depression is a yearly recurring depression. This type of depression is an involuntary emotional reaction to past loss or trauma related to the anniversary of its occurrence (such as an abortion, miscarriage, house fire, death of a spouse or child, etc.). It lasts for a limited period of time with the onset triggered by memories.

Write from the Heart

Do you, or someone you know, experience anniversary depression? What recurring memory of the event brings on the depression? How long did it take for you to recognize what was causing the depression?

....

....

....

....

....

....

What specific things can you do to encourage yourself or someone else who struggles with anniversary depression?

....

....

....

....

....

....

....

GUIDED BY THE SPIRIT

The Holy Spirit indwells every Christian. He is God's presence within the believer. It is through having Him that you actually have the power of Christ to meet every trial and overcome every difficulty. Even in the depths of your despair and in the darkness of your depression, God is with you, for He is *in* you by His Spirit. He helps you in your weakness, and He intercedes for you.

To overcome your depression, look to the Holy Spirit for power and for help.

> *"The Spirit helps us in our weakness. We do not know what we ought to pray for, but the Spirit himself intercedes for us through wordless groans.*
>
> *And he who searches our hearts knows the mind of the Spirit, because the Spirit intercedes for God's people in accordance with the will of God."*
>
> ROMANS 8:26–27

Even in the depths of your despair and in the darkness of your depression, God is with you.

Discussion/Application Questions

1. Psalm 46:1 says, "God is our refuge and strength, an ever-present help in trouble." What are common "refuges" that people run to when they are depressed or angry?

2. Who or what do you typically run to when you're depressed or angry? What are you hoping to find?

3. How do you relate to God when you're depressed? In what ways, if any, does this differ from times when you're *not* depressed?

....

....

....

....

....

....

....

....

4. Read Psalm 121:1–6. What do you find encouraging from this passage? What does God promise He will do?

....

....

....

....

....

....

....

....

5. Read Psalm 121:1–6 two or three times. Then, in your own words, write down what this passage means for you when you face difficult times in your life.

....

....

....

....

....

....

....

....

....

....

....

....

....

....

....

....

Notes

Notes

"Now may the Lord of peace himself give you
peace at all times and in every way."
2 Thessalonians 3:16

SESSION 5

BIBLICAL STEPS TO SOLUTION
PART 2

"Even though I walk through the darkest valley, I will fear no evil, for you are with me; your rod and your staff, they comfort me."

PSALM 23:4

A Positive Perspective on Depression

When you are walking through the dark valley of depression, knowing God's Word and purposes in suffering can make a real difference in your life. What do you need to know from His Word?

- **You need to see your life from God's perspective.**

  He cares about you and has positive plans for your life.

  The Lord says, "For I know the plans I have for you . . . plans to prosper you and not to harm you, plans to give you hope and a future" (Jeremiah 29:11).

- **You need to know that God has a purpose for everything He allows in your life.**

  Nothing in your life occurs that has not first been filtered through God's fingers. If God permits it, He will use it for your good and for His glory.

  Romans 8:28 says, "We know that in all things God works for the good of those who love him, who have been called according to his purpose."

- **You need to know that there will be times when your heart will be pressed down, but also times of restoration because God is a healer of broken hearts.**

  He heals us when we give our heart to Him. And, He knows how to restore our joy.

  "He heals the brokenhearted and binds up their wounds" (Psalm 147:3).

- **You need to know that no matter how great your despondency, God can open your eyes to His unique design for your life.**

  Just as storms replenish the dry, parched soil, giving birth to new life, the storms in your life can revitalize your relationship with the Lord and give birth to personal growth beyond what you could ever imagine.

  Psalm 119:67 says, "Before I was afflicted I went astray, but now I obey your word."

Suffering and depression are not purposeless. God can use your pain to accomplish His purposes. The apostle Paul explains that he was "hard pressed on every side, but not crushed; perplexed, but not in despair; persecuted, but not abandoned; struck down, but not destroyed" (2 Corinthians 4:8–9). He did not lose heart because he kept an eternal perspective on life.

"Therefore we do not lose heart. Though outwardly we are wasting away, yet inwardly we are being renewed day by day. For our light and momentary troubles are achieving for us an eternal glory that far outweighs them all. So we fix our eyes not on what is seen, but on what is unseen, since what is seen is temporary, but what is unseen is eternal."

2 CORINTHIANS 4:16–18

Write from the Heart

Read Revelation 21:1–5, a passage about heaven. What does God promise He will do in this passage?

....

....

....

....

....

....

How does keeping an eternal perspective on things influence your current suffering?

....

....

....

....

....

....

What Is God's Purpose for Depression?

God has a purpose for everything that you experience. Even the storm clouds in your life are useful in the hands of God. Just as storms replenish dry and parched ground and give birth to flowers and new life in the spring, so the storms in your life can revitalize your relationship with God and give birth to abundant spiritual fruit.

The Lord can use your suffering and depression to accomplish many purposes . . .

- **To develop obedience**

  "Before I was afflicted I went astray, but now I obey your word" (Psalm 119:67).

- **To reveal your weakness and Christ's power**

  "[The Lord said] 'My grace is sufficient for you, for my power is made perfect in weakness.' Therefore I [Paul] will boast all the more gladly about my weaknesses, so that Christ's power may rest on me" (2 Corinthians 12:9).

- **To develop perseverance, character, and hope**

  "Not only so, but we also glory in our sufferings, because we know that suffering produces perseverance; perseverance [produces] character; and character [produces] hope. And hope does not put us to shame, because God's love has been poured out into our hearts through the Holy Spirit, who has been given to us" (Romans 5:3–5).

- **To make you more teachable**

    "It was good for me to be afflicted so that I might learn your decrees" (Psalm 119:71).

- **To give you a desire for eternal glory rather than temporal pleasures.**

    "I consider that our present sufferings are not worth comparing with the glory that will be revealed in us" (Romans 8:18).

- **To test the genuineness of your faith**

    "In all this you greatly rejoice, though now for a little while you may have had to suffer grief in all kinds of trials. These have come so that the proven genuineness of your faith—of greater worth than gold, which perishes even though refined by fire—may result in praise, glory and honor when Jesus Christ is revealed" (1 Peter 1:6–7).

- **To develop maturity**

    "Consider it pure joy, my brothers and sisters, whenever you face trials of many kinds, because you know that the testing of your faith produces perseverance. Let perseverance finish its work so that you may be mature and complete, not lacking anything" (James 1:2–4).

- **To cause you to rely on God instead of your own strength and resources**

    "We were under great pressure, far beyond our ability to endure, so that we despaired of life itself. Indeed, we felt we had received the sentence of death. But this happened that we might not rely on ourselves but on God, who raises the dead" (2 Corinthians 1:8–9).

- **To increase your compassion and understanding for others**

  "Praise be to the God and Father of our Lord Jesus Christ, the Father of compassion and the God of all comfort, who comforts us in all our troubles, so that we can comfort those in any trouble with the comfort we ourselves receive from God" (2 Corinthians 1:3–4).

Even the storm clouds in your life are useful in the hands of God.

Write from the Heart

Which of the purposes for suffering resonate most with you? What do you think the Lord is currently trying to teach you in your struggles?

Bringing Light into the Darkness

The Word of God reveals many purposes for your suffering. The truth in God's Word gives meaning to your suffering. It also helps combat the fears and lies that you may believe and tell yourself. One helpful exercise to fight these lies is to write out your thoughts, then, as your rebuttal, write out what God says. When difficult thoughts enter your mind, simply replace them with the light of truth from His Word.

*"Your word is a lamp for my feet,
a light on my path."*

PSALM 119:105

- *Darkness:* "I cannot escape this darkness."

  Light: "The Lord will replace the darkness with His light."

  God's Word says: "My God turns my darkness into light" (Psalm 18:28).

- *Darkness:* "I have no refuge, no safe haven."

  Light: "The Lord will be my refuge."

  God's Word says: "Keep me safe, my God, for in you I take refuge" (Psalm 16:1).

- *Darkness:* "I feel like I'm in too much trouble."

   Light: "The Lord is my help in trouble."

   God's Word says: "God is our refuge and strength, an ever-present help in trouble" (Psalm 46:1).

- *Darkness:* "I can't help feeling so restless."

   Light: "My God gives my soul rest."

   God's Word says: "Truly my soul finds rest in God; my salvation comes from him" (Psalm 62:1).

- *Darkness:* "I can't see the path I should take."

   Light: "The Lord will direct my path."

   God's Word says: "Trust in the Lord with all your heart and lean not on your own understanding; in all your ways submit to him, and he will make your paths straight" (Proverbs 3:5–6).

- *Darkness:* "My burden is too heavy to bear."

   Light: "The Lord is my burden bearer."

   God's Word says: "Praise be to the Lord, to God our Savior, who daily bears our burdens" (Psalm 68:19).

- *Darkness:* "I'm afraid to be around people."

   Light: "The Lord will give me strength to be around people."

   God's Word says: "The Lord is my light and my salvation—whom shall I fear? The Lord is the stronghold of my life—of whom shall I be afraid?" (Psalm 27:1).

Write from the Heart

What negative thoughts often play over and over in your mind?
Write down a negative thought ("darkness"), then a truth from God's
Word ("light").

Darkness (Negative Thought): ....

....

....

Light (Truth from God's Word): ....

....

....

Darkness (Negative Thought): ....

....

....

Light (Truth from God's Word): ....

....

....

Discussion/Application Questions

1. Describe the difference between what society says about the purpose of suffering and what the Bible says about the purpose of suffering. What does society say you should do with your suffering, and what does the Bible say you should do with it?

    ....

    ....

    ....

    ....

    ....

    ....

2. When growing up, what did you learn from family, friends, etc. about managing emotional pain? How has what you learned then carried over into the present and influenced the way you deal with pain now?

    ....

    ....

    ....

    ....

    ....

    ....

3. Read Isaiah 53:3–12 and 1 Peter 3:18. Christ's suffering had purpose—to save you and bring you to God. Reflect on the suffering of Christ for a moment. What does it mean to you to know that Jesus suffered for you and fully understands what you're going through?

Notes

"*Now may the Lord of peace himself give you
peace at all times and in every way.*"
2 Thessalonians 3:16

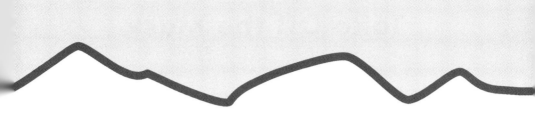

SESSION 6

BIBLICAL STEPS TO SOLUTION
PART 3

"Praise be to the God and Father of our Lord Jesus Christ, the Father of compassion and the God of all comfort, who comforts us in all our troubles, so that we can comfort those in any trouble with the comfort we ourselves receive from God."

2 CORINTHIANS 1:3–4

Take Off the Mask

As we go through painful events, we can sometimes sweep them under the rug, refuse to acknowledge them, or choose to see them only in a light we can accept. When we ignore the pain, we fail to grieve our hurts and losses. By wearing a mask, we try to protect our heart and hide who we really are and what we don't want to face. But this kind of masquerade blocks maturity and the ability to have intimacy with God and others.

Don't ever fear allowing God to help you see the reality of your pain and how He has been working through the painful experiences in your life.

*"You delight in truth in the inward being,
and you teach me wisdom in
the secret heart."*

PSALM 51:6 ESV

Write from the Heart

What emotions do you find most difficult to bring to the Lord? Why? What prevents you from being fully open with Him?

Learn to Bring Depression to the Lord

When you are weary, when life isn't worth living, when hope seems elusive, what do you need to know? You need to know your Burden Bearer—you need to know Jesus. He is the Shepherd of your soul. His compassionate comfort extends to all those who have lost hope. He knows and understands everything you're going through; therefore, you don't have to wear a mask with Him.

For the weary and burdened, Jesus invites you to come to Him:

> *"Come to me, all you who are*
> *weary and burdened, and*
> *I will give you rest."*
>
> Matthew 11:28

When darkness falls into your life, you can easily become consumed with the situation that causes the darkness. At those times, you may have difficulty seeing all that God wants you to see. During those days when you are shrouded in darkness, you must not trust in your own perspective. Instead, you need to see life from God's perspective. This requires you to confront your losses, offer your heart to God, and allow Him to shed His light on your life.

> *"Let the one who walks in the dark, who has no light,*
> *trust in the name of the Lord and rely on their God."*
>
> Isaiah 50:10

The following acrostic will help you *CONQUER* your depression.

CONFRONT any loss in your life, allowing yourself to grieve and be healed.

"[There is] a time to weep and a time to laugh, a time to mourn and a time to dance" (Ecclesiastes 3:4).

OFFER your heart to God for cleansing, and confess your sins.

"If we claim to be without sin, we deceive ourselves and the truth is not in us. If we confess our sins, he is faithful and just and will forgive us our sins and purify us from all unrighteousness" (1 John 1:8–9).

NURTURE thoughts that focus on God's great love for you.

"I have loved you with an everlasting love; I have drawn you with unfailing kindness" (Jeremiah 31:3).

QUIT negative thinking and negative self-talk.

"Finally, brothers and sisters, whatever is true, whatever is noble, whatever is right, whatever is pure, whatever is lovely, whatever is admirable—if anything is excellent or praiseworthy—think about such things" (Philippians 4:8).

UNDERSTAND God's eternal purpose for allowing personal loss and heartache.

"We know that in all things God works for the good of those who love him, who have been called according to his purpose" (Romans 8:28).

*E*XCHANGE your hurt and anger for the choice to give thanks (even when you don't feel thankful).

"Give thanks in all circumstances; for this is God's will for you in Christ Jesus" (1 Thessalonians 5:18).

*R*EMEMBER that God is sovereign over your life, and He promises hope for your future.

"'I know the plans I have for you,' declares the Lord, 'plans to prosper you and not to harm you, plans to give you hope and a future'" (Jeremiah 29:11).

We need to see life from God's perspective.

Write from the Heart

In Jeremiah 31:3, God says, "I have loved you with an everlasting love; I have drawn you with unfailing kindness." Make a list of a few other verses or stories from the Bible about God's love for you. How do they give you meaning and purpose when you're struggling with depression or suffering?

How You Can Help

When you have depressed loved ones in your life, you want to do something that will make a difference. The question is *what?* There are a variety of things you can do to reach out to a friend but whatever you do, avoiding your friend is not an option.

Find ways to show you care. Plan a fun activity with them, exercise with them, or help them find a hobby. Invite them to outside events or to run errands with you. Because of their tendency to withdraw and isolate, help them get involved in activities—not just be a spectator. Realize that you may be their only lifeline of hope—and they need to stay connected. Do what you would want someone else to do for you if you struggled with depression.

"Do to others as you
would have them
do to you."

Luke 6:31

- **Learn all you can about depression**: read books, watch videos, attend seminars.

  "Apply your heart to instruction and your ears to words of knowledge" (Proverbs 23:12).

- **Talk about depression.** Talking helps remove the stigma of depression.

  "A word fitly spoken is like apples of gold in settings of silver" (Proverbs 25:11 NKJV).

- **If suicide is a concern, ask, "Are you thinking about hurting yourself?"** Take all threats of suicide and self-injury seriously.

  "The tongue has the power of life and death" (Proverbs 18:21).

- **Be an accountability partner.** Let them know that you'll be there for them.

   "Two are better than one, because they have a good return for their labor" (Ecclesiastes 4:9).

- **Contact them regularly:** frequent phone calls, texts, e-mails.

   "Encourage one another and build each other up" (1 Thessalonians 5:11).

- **Listen to them and hear their pain.** Listening affirms their value.

   "Everyone should be quick to listen, slow to speak and slow to become angry" (James 1:19).

- **Verbally encourage them**, sincerely and often.

   "Do not let any unwholesome talk come out of your mouths, but only what is helpful for building others up according to their needs, that it may benefit those who listen" (Ephesians 4:29).

- **Realize the power of touch:** a hand on the shoulder or a hug.

   "Greet one another with a kiss of love" (1 Peter 5:14).

- **Give them inspirational praise music to lift their spirits.** Music is therapeutic.

   "Speaking to one another with psalms, hymns, and songs from the Spirit" (Ephesians 5:19).

- **Bring laughter into their lives:** fun cards, videos, movies, and people.

   "A cheerful heart is good medicine"(Proverbs 17:22).

- **Enlist help from other family and friends.** Be specific about your concerns.

  "Carry each other's burdens, and in this way you will fulfill the law of Christ"(Galatians 6:2).

- **Pray for them regularly**. Pray for God to heal, teach, comfort, and guide them amid their pain.

  "And pray in the Spirit on all occasions with all kinds of prayers and requests. With this in mind, be alert and always keep on praying for all the Lord's people" (Ephesians 6:18).

Write from the Heart

Think of someone you know who may be struggling with depression. List five specific things you can do to help them.

(1) ....

....

....

(2) ....

....

....

(3) ....

....

....

(4) ....

....

....

(5) ....

....

....

Do's and Don'ts for Family and Friends

Sometimes when a loved one is struggling, you may become impatient because you want them to feel better *now*. In your impatience, you might say the wrong thing and worsen the problem. The Bible gives numerous instructions about the importance of speaking and listening well.

"The one who has knowledge uses words with restraint, and whoever has understanding is even-tempered."

PROVERBS 17:27

Don't say: "You shouldn't feel that way."

Do Say: "I care about what you are feeling."

- Ask, "Would you like to share your feelings with me?"

- Say, "If ever you want to talk, I'm here for you."

  "The purposes of a person's heart are deep waters, but one who has insight draws them out" (Proverbs 20:5).

Don't say: "You need to quit taking that medicine."

Do Say: "Not all medicines work the same for everyone. I'll go with you to get a thorough medical evaluation so that the doctor will make sure the medicine is working for you."

- Talk specifically to a competent doctor who specializes in depression.

- Don't be afraid to get a second opinion.

  "Plans fail for lack of counsel, but with many advisers they succeed" (Proverbs 15:22).

Don't say: "You just need to pray more."

Do Say: "I'm praying for you, and I'm going to keep praying."

- Pray with them, and tell them you are praying for them.

- Ask specifically, "How can I pray for you today?"

  "Far be it from me that I should sin against the LORD by failing to pray for you" (1 Samuel 12:23).

Don't say: "You just need to read the Bible more."

Do Say: "There are several passages in the Bible that have given me much hope, and I've written them out for you. May I share them with you?"

- Give them hope-filled Scriptures to read three times a day: after waking up, midday, and bedtime (Jeremiah 29:11; Psalm 130:5).

- Help them memorize Scripture (Philippians 4:6–8; 4:13; 4:19).

  "I rise before dawn and cry for help; I have put my hope in your word" (Psalm 119:147).

Don't say: "You need to go to church."

Do Say: "I'm involved in a church that has really helped me out during tough times. I would love for you to come with me next Sunday, and afterward we can have lunch together."

- Invite them to come to church or small group Bible study with you.

- Offer to give them a ride to church.

  "Let us consider how we may spur one another on toward love and good deeds, not giving up meeting together, as some are in the habit of doing, but encouraging one another" (Hebrews 10:24–25).

Don't say: "Snap out of it! Get over it!"

Do Say: "I'm going to stick with you, and we'll get through this together."

- Admit, "I don't know everything I wish I knew, but I'm willing to help."

- Say, "I'm not going to leave you."

  "There is a friend who sticks closer than a brother" (Proverbs 18:24).

Write from the Heart

Words can build up and bless others (Ephesians 4:29). Describe a time when someone encouraged you with their words, either spoken or written. What impact did their words have on your situation and on your life? If you had a chance to say something to bless and encourage that person today, what would it be?

Discussion/Application Questions

1. Over the past six sessions, how has your understanding of depression changed as a result of this study? Describe one or two key takeaways the Lord has revealed to you about handling depression.

....

....

....

....

....

2. Take a moment and list some of the good things God has done in your life during times of suffering and depression. What did He teach you about yourself, about life, and about Himself during those times?

....

....

....

....

....

....

3. Describe at least one habit you will begin, change, or stop to handle depression more effectively.

4. Psalm 68:19 says, "Praise be to the Lord, to God our Savior, who daily bears our burdens." Take some time to praise God for *daily* bearing your burdens and walking with you through this study. Write down all the reasons for which you can praise and thank God.

Notes

"Now may the Lord of peace himself give you
peace at all times and in every way."
2 Thessalonians 3:16

Endnotes

1. *Merriam-Webster's Collegiate Dictionary* (electronic edition) (Merriam-Webster, 2001).

2. *Merriam-Webster's Collegiate Dictionary.*

3. James Strong, *Strong's Greek Lexicon* (electronic edition; Online Bible Millennium Edition v. 1.13) (Timnathserah Inc., July 6, 2002).

4. H. Norman Wright, *Beating the Blues: Overcoming Depression and Stress* (Ventura, CA: Regal, 1988), 9.

5. *Merriam-Webster's Collegiate Dictionary.*

6. *Merriam-Webster's Collegiate Dictionary.*

7. Stephen A. Grunlan and Daniel H. Lambrides, *Healing Relationships: A Christian's Manual for Lay Counseling* (Camp Hill, PA: Christian Publications, 1984), 121.

8. A disorder means that a person's normal functioning of life is impaired. A person with a depressive disorder has "clinical depression."

9. A disorder means that a person's normal functioning of life is impaired. A person with a depressive disorder has "clinical depression."

10. Archibald D. Hart, *Counseling the Depressed*, vol. 5, Resources for Christian Counseling, ed. Gary R. Collins (Dallas: Word, 1987), 34.

11. "Texas mother charged with killing her 5 children." June 21, 2001, http://www.cnn.com/2001/US/06/20/children.killed/index.html.

12. Archibald D. Hart, "The Psychopathology of Postpartum Disorders," *Christian Counseling Today* 10, no. 4 (2002): 16–17.

13. DSM-IV TR, 422–3; Michael R. Lyles, "Psychiatric Aspects of Postpartum Mood Disorders," *Christian Counseling Today* 10, no. 4 (2002): 19.

14. DSM-IV TR, 422.

15. Timothy Roche, "Andrea Yates: More to the Story." March 18, 2002, http://content.time.com/time/nation/article/0,8599,218445,00.html.

16. Archibald Hart and Catherine Hart Weber, *Unveiling Depression in Women: A Practical Guide to Understanding and Overcoming Depression*, (Grand Rapids: Fleming H. Revell, 2002), 55.

17. Hart and Weber, 56.

18. Michael Lyles, *Women and Depression, Extraordinary Women*, EW 301, VHS (Forest, VA: American Association of Christian Counselors, n.d.).

19. James W. Jefferson, "My Hippocampus Is Bigger than Yours!" *Geriatric Times* 1, no. 4 (2000), http://www.geriatrictimes.com/g001220.html.

20. Ray Burwick, *The Menace Within: Hurt or Anger?* (Birmingham, AL: Ray Burwick, 1985), 18; Gary D. Chapman, *The Other Side of Love: Handling Anger in a Godly Way* (Chicago: Moody, 1999), 17–18.

21. June Hunt, *Anger: Facing the Fire Within.* (California: Aspire Press, 2013), 12–13.

22. *The Andrea Yates Story,* VHS (A & E Television Networks, 2003).

23. Roche, "Andrea Yates: More to the Story."

24. Roche, "Andrea Yates: More to the Story."

25. Hart and Weber, 180–81; "Symptoms." SADAssociation, http://www.sada.org.uk/symptoms.htm.

HOPE FOR THE HEART
Biblically Based Studies on Everyday Issues
6-Session Bible Studies

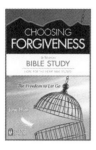

CHOOSING FORGIVENESS
Learn how you can be an expression of God's grace by forgiving others and find the freedom He intended you to have.
ISBN: 9781628623840

DEALING WITH ANGER
Have you ever reacted rashly out of anger—and lived to regret it? You can learn to keep your anger under control and learn how to act rather than react.
ISBN: 9781628623871

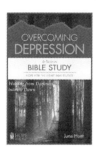

OVERCOMING DEPRESSION
Can anything dispel the darkness of depression? The answer is yes! Let God lead you through the storm and into the light.
ISBN: 9781628623901

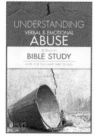

UNDERSTANDING VERBAL AND EMOTIONAL ABUSE
You can learn biblical truths and practical "how to's" for stopping the pain of abuse and for restoring peace in all your relationships.
ISBN: 9781628623932

HANDLING STRESS
Discover biblical approaches to handling stress. God wants to be your source of calm in stressful situations.
ISBN: 9781628623963

FINDING SELF-WORTH IN CHRIST
Learn to leave behind feelings of worthlessness, and experience the worth you have in the eyes of your heavenly Father.
ISBN: 9781628623994

www.HendricksonRose.com • www.AspirePress.com